WE WISH YOU
A MERRY CHRISTMAS

SONGS OF THE SEASON
FOR YOUNG PEOPLE

ARRANGED BY
DAN FOX

THE METROPOLITAN MUSEUM OF ART
NEW YORK

ARCADE PUBLISHING
NEW YORK

LITTLE, BROWN AND COMPANY

Copyright © 1989 by The Metropolitan Museum of Art
All rights reserved, including the right to reproduce this book or portions thereof in any form.
Published by The Metropolitan Museum of Art, New York, and Arcade Publishing, Inc., New York,
a Little, Brown company.
Published simultaneously in Canada by Little, Brown & Company (Canada) Limited.

Produced by the Department of Special Publications,
The Metropolitan Museum of Art
Photography by The Metropolitan Museum of Art Photograph Studio
Music engraved by W. R. Music Service, New York
Printed and bound in Japan by Dai Nippon Printing Co., Ltd.
Designed by Miriam Berman

Library of Congress Catalog Card Number 89-84225
Library of Congress Cataloging-in-Publication Data is available.

ISBN 0-87099-552-9 (MMA)
ISBN 1-55970-043-2 (Arcade)

1 3 5 7 9 10 8 6 4 2

CONTENTS

The Christmas Tree.
J. Alden Weir,
American,
1852–1919.
Oil on canvas, 1890.

4

PREFACE

WE WISH YOU A MERRY CHRISTMAS presents twenty-five classic holiday songs from England, Wales, France, Germany, and America. The music dates from the Middle Ages to the twentieth century and the songs express the many moods of the Christmas season: from solemn to festive, from gentle to triumphant, from quiet to exuberant. The musical arrangements are simple and easy to follow, suitable for beginning to intermediate musicians.

All of the songs in the book have been imaginatively coupled with one or more works from the collections of The Metropolitan Museum of Art in New York—paintings, drawings, lithographs, woodcuts, tapestries, sculpture, stained glass, tiles, and illuminated manuscripts. The art spans more than five hundred years and comes from many countries—Germany, France, Italy, Austria, England, Switzerland, Egypt, Belgium, Holland, and America. It ranges from paintings of the Nativity by unknown Renaissance artists to masterpieces of the same subject by Hieronymus Bosch and François Boucher; from sixth-century Egyptian textiles to elaborate silk embroideries made in England eleven centuries later; and from simple medieval woodcuts to colorful lithographs of the twentieth century.

It is our hope that the diversity of the art, the selection of the songs, and the simplicity of the arrangements will enhance the enjoyment of the holiday season.

A NOTE ON THE MUSIC

Each of the songs includes guitar chords that can be used for easy accompaniment; a fingering chart appears on page 80. When an arrangement is in a key that is awkward for the guitar, capo instructions and alternate chords are provided. After the capo is in place, the song should be played using the chords that appear in parentheses.

The music is suitable not only for piano and guitar, but also for other C instruments, such as the violin, flute, and recorder. Players of these instruments should read the highest notes in the upper staff.

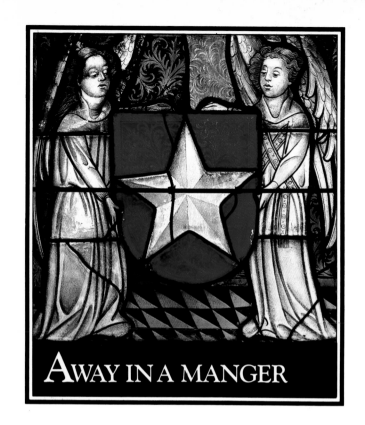

Away in a Manger

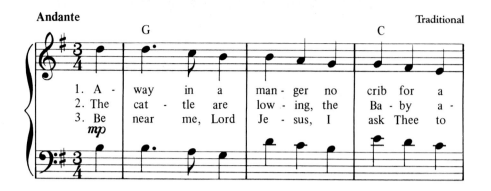

Andante
Traditional

1. A - way in a man - ger no crib for a
2. The cat - tle are low - ing, the Ba - by a -
3. Be near me, Lord Je - sus, I ask Thee to

mp

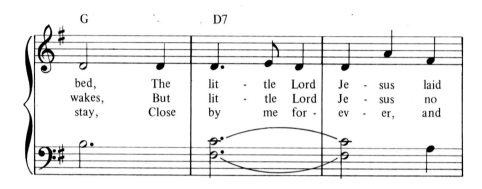

bed, The lit - tle Lord Je - sus laid
wakes, But lit - tle Lord Je - sus no
stay, Close by me for - ev - er, and

down His sweet head. The stars in the sky_____ looked down where He
cry - ing He makes. I love Thee, Lord Je - sus, look down from the
love me, I pray; Bless all the dear chil - dren in Thy ten - der

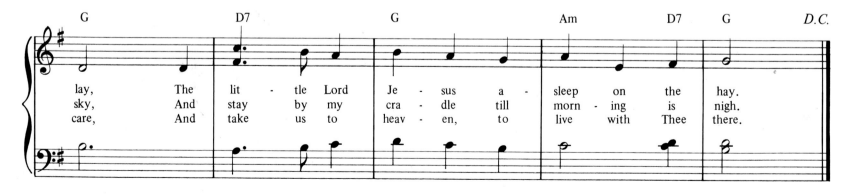

lay, The lit - tle Lord Je - sus a - sleep on the hay.
sky, And stay by my cra - dle till morn - ing is nigh.
care, And take us to heav - en, to live with Thee there.

Details of two stained-glass windows from the Carmelite Church at Boppard-on-the-Rhine. German, 1440–46.

7

O LITTLE TOWN OF BETHLEHEM

Words by Phillips Brooks
Music by Lewis H. Redner

Moderately

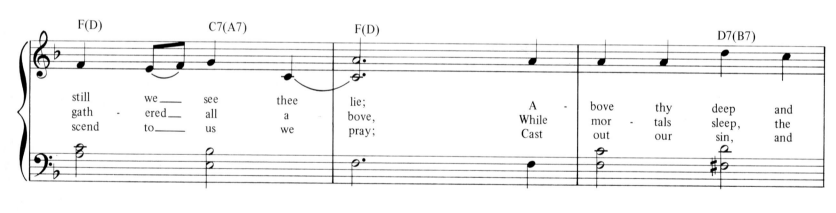

F(D)*   Bb(G)   Gm(Em)

1. O lit - tle town of Beth - le - hem, How
2. For Christ is born of Mar - y, And
3. O ho - ly Child of Beth - le - hem, De -

F(D)   C7(A7)   F(D)   D7(B7)

still we see thee lie; A - bove thy deep and
gath - ered all a - bove, While mor - tals sleep, the
scend to us we pray; Cast out our sin, and

Gm(Em)   F(D)   C7(A7)   F(D)

dream - less sleep, The si - lent stars go by. Yet
an - gels keep Their watch of won - d'ring love. O
en - ter in, Be born to us to - day. We

*Guitar: Capo 3rd fret

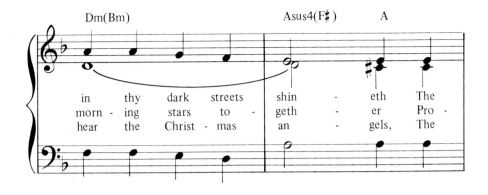

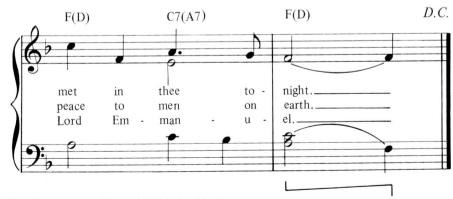

Detail from a painting, *Virgin and Child*, by Joos Van Cleve, Flemish, active by 1507, d. 1540/41. Tempera and oil on wood.

SILENT NIGHT

Words adapted from the German of Joseph Mohr
Music by Franz Grüber

Quietly

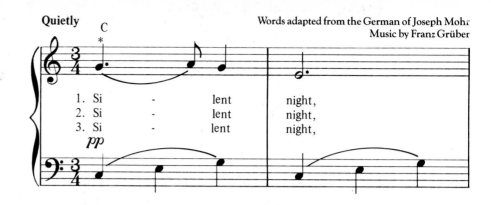

1. Si - lent night,
2. Si - lent night,
3. Si - lent night,

pp

ho - ly night,
ho - ly night,
ho - ly night,

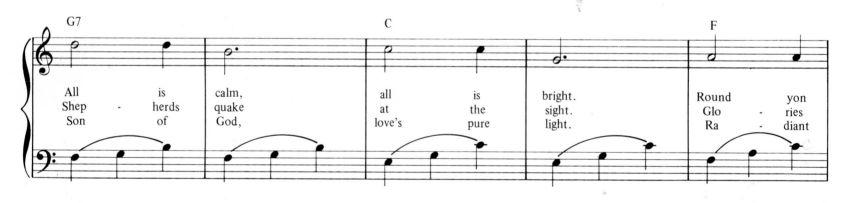

All - is calm, all is bright. Round yon
Shep - herds quake God, at love's is the pure sight. light. Glo - ries
Son of God, the bright. sight. Ra - diant

Vir - gin Moth - er and Child, Ho - ly In - fant so
stream from heav - en a - far, Heav'n - ly hosts sing
beams from Thy ho - ly face, With the dawn of

*For a very nice "music box" effect, play both hands an octave higher.

(Please turn the page.)

Detail of an engraving from *Ethica naturalis, seu documenta moralia,*
written by Christopher Weigel (German). Published in Nuremberg, ca. 1700.

The Adoration of the Shepherds. Marcellus Coffermans, Flemish, active between 1549 and 1570. Tempera and oil on wood.

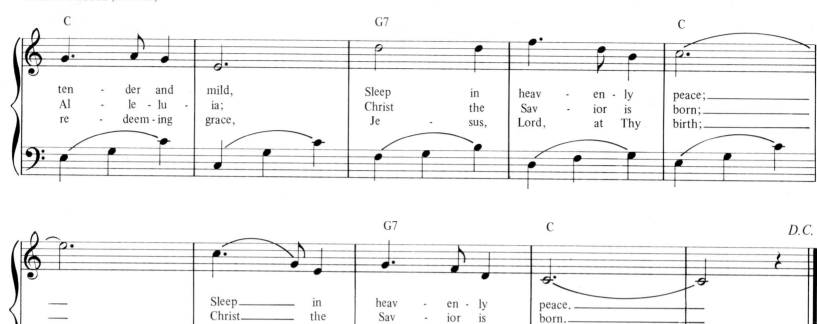

ten - der and mild, / Al - le - lu - ia; / re - deem -ing grace,
Sleep in heav - en - ly peace; / Christ the Sav - ior is born; / Je - sus, Lord, at Thy birth;

Sleep in heav - en - ly peace. / Christ the Sav - ior is born. / Je - sus, Lord, at Thy birth.

D.C.

The Nativity. Workshop of Fra Angelico, Italian (Florentine), active by 1417, d. 1455. Tempera and gold on wood.

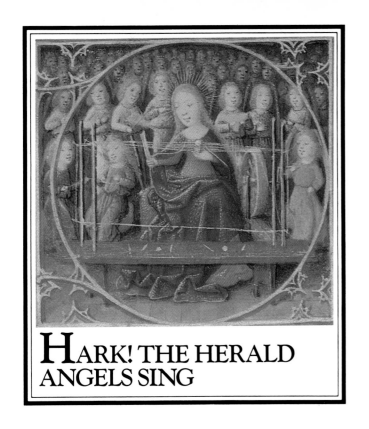

HARK! THE HERALD ANGELS SING

Words by Charles Wesley
Music by Felix Mendelssohn

Firmly

1. Hark! the her - ald an - gels sing,____
2. Hail the heav'n - born Prince of Peace!____

Glo - ry to the new - born King!
Hail the Son of Right - eous - ness!

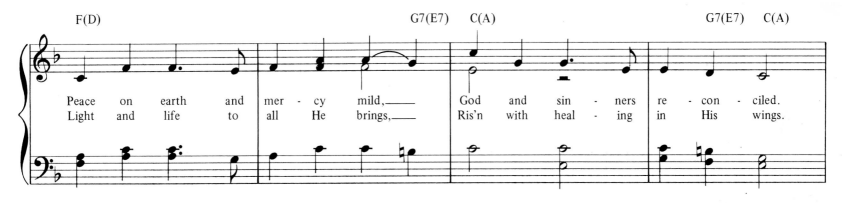

Peace on earth and mer - cy mild,____ God and sin - ners re - con - ciled.
Light and life to all He brings,____ Ris'n with heal - ing in His wings.

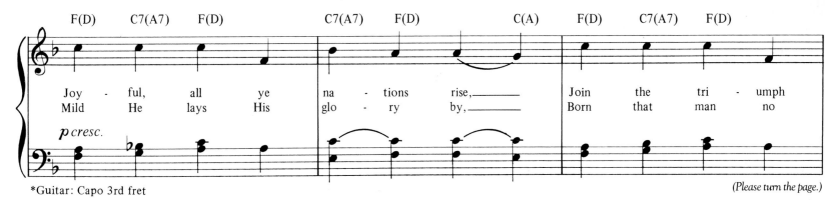

Joy - ful, all ye na - tions rise,____ Join the tri - umph
Mild He lays His glo - ry by,____ Born that man no

*Guitar: Capo 3rd fret

(Please turn the page.)

Detail of a manuscript illumination from a *Book of Hours*
made for Charles of France, Duke of Normandy. French, 1465.

The Annunciation: Archangel Gabriel. Manuscript illumination from a *Book of Hours* made for Charles of France, Duke of Normandy. French, 1465.

14

Illustration from *Nobilità di Dame . . .chiamoto Il Ballarino,* written by Fabritio Caroso da Sermoneta. Published by Presso il Muschio, Venice, 1605.

DECK THE HALLS

Brightly, with spirit

Welsh traditional

1. Deck the halls with boughs of hol - ly,
2. See the blaz - ing Yule be - fore us,
3. Fast a - way the old year pass - es,

Fa la la la la la la la la.

'Tis the sea - son to be jol - ly,
Strike the harp and join the cho - rus,
Hail the new, ye lads and lass - es,

Fa la la la la la la la la.

Don we now our gay ap - par - el,
Fol - low me in mer - ry mea - sure,
Sing we joy - ous all to - geth - er,

Fa la la la la la la.

Detail of a color lithograph by Mela Koehler (Austrian, 1885–1960), published by the Wiener Werkstätte, ca. 1908–14.

Detail from a magazine cover by Louis Rhead (American, 1857–1926) for *Harper's Bazaar*, Christmas 1894.

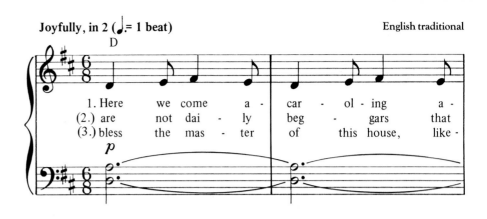

Joyfully, in 2 (♩.= 1 beat) English traditional

1. Here we come a-car-ol-ing a-
(2.) are not dai-ly beg-gars that
(3.) bless the mas-ter of this house, like-

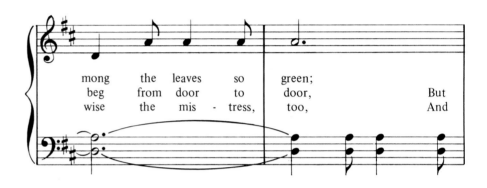

mong the leaves so green; But
beg from door to door, And
wise the mis-tress, too,

HERE WE
COME A-CAROLING

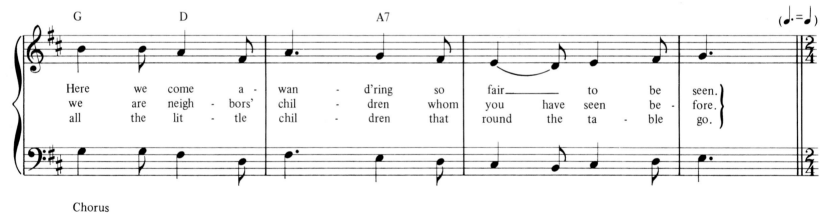

Here we come a-wan-d'ring so fair_____ to be seen.
we are neigh-bors' chil-dren whom you have seen be-fore.
all the lit-tle chil-dren that round the ta-ble go.

Chorus

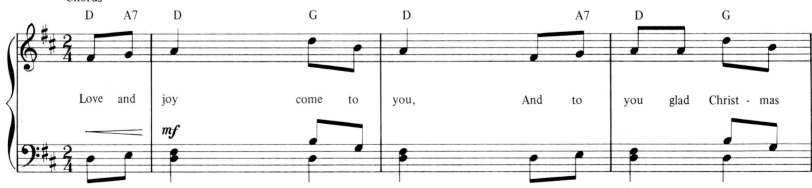

Love and joy come to you, And to you glad Christ-mas

Playing Under the Windows (detail). Cecil Aldin, British, 1870–1935.
Illustration from *Old Christmas* by Washington Irving, published by Hodder & Stoughton, London, 1908.

18

too, And God bless you and send you a Hap - py New

Year, And God send you a Hap - py New

1.&2. | D.C. | 3.

Year. 2. We 3. God

Year.

Details of illustrations by Maurice Boutet de Monvel (French, 1851–1913) from *Vieilles chansons et rondes pour les petits enfants*. Published by Librairie Plon, Paris, 1883.

TOYLAND

Gently flowing

Words by Glen MacDonough
Music by Victor Herbert

F(D)*

Toy - land,

pp

Fmaj7(Dmaj7)

Toy - land,

Gm7(Em7)   C7(A7)   Fdim(G♯dim)   F(D)   B♭(G)

Lit - tle   girl   and   boy   land,   While   you

F(D)   Dm(Bm)   G7(E7)

dwell   with - in   it____   You   are   ev - er   hap - py

*Guitar: Capo 3rd fret

(Please turn the page.)

Detail of a color lithograph by Suzi Singer-Schinnerl (Austrian, 1895–1965), published by the Wiener Werkstätte, ca. 1912.

Illustration by Wyndham
Payne (British) from *The
Mysterious Toyshop, A Fairy Tale*
by Cyril W. Beaumont.
Published in London, 1924.

Illustration by Wyndham
Payne (British) from *The
Mysterious Toyshop, A Fairy Tale*
by Cyril W. Beaumont.
Published in London, 1924.

THE FRIENDLY BEASTS

Gently   Traditional

F(D)*

1. Je - sus our broth - er,
2. "I," said our the don - key,
3. "I," said the cow, all

p - mp

C7(A7)   F(D)

kind gy and good, was
shag - gy and brown, "I
white and red, "I

Bb(G)   F(D)

hum - bly born in a sta - ble rude, And the
car - ried His moth - er up hill and down; I
gave Him my man - ger for a bed; I

C7(A7)   F(D)   C7(A7)   F(D)

friend - ly beasts a - round Him stood,
car - ried her safe - ly to Beth - le - hem town."
gave Him my hay to pil - low His head."

*Guitar: Capo 3rd fret

The Creation of the Animals. Detail of a stained-glass panel. Swiss, 1694.

24

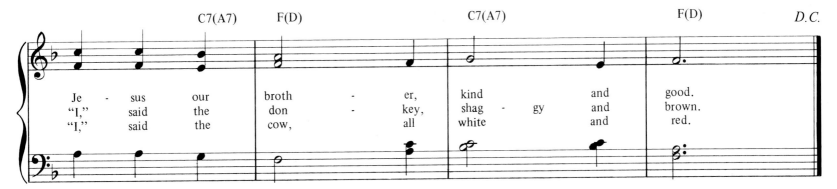

	C7(A7)	F(D)		C7(A7)	F(D)	D.C.

Je - sus our broth - er, kind and good.
"I," said the don - key, shag - gy and brown.
"I," said the cow, all white and red.

Additional verses:

4.
"I," said the sheep with curly horn,
"I gave Him my wool for His blanket warm;
He wore my coat on Christmas morn.
I," said the sheep with curly horn.

5.
"I," said the dove from the rafters high,
"Cooed Him to sleep that He should not cry;
We cooed Him to sleep, my mate and I.
I," said the dove from the rafters high.

6.
"I," said the camel, yellow and black,
"Over the desert, upon my back,
I brought Him a gift in the Wise Men's pack.
I," said the camel, yellow and black.

7.
Thus every beast by some good spell,
In the stable dark was glad to tell
Of the gift he gave Emmanuel,
The gift he gave Emmanuel.

The Nativity (detail). Antoniazzo Romano (Antonio di Benedetto Aquilio), Italian (Roman), active by 1452, d. by 1512. Tempera on wood.

With spirit

Words and music by James Pierpont

JINGLE BELLS

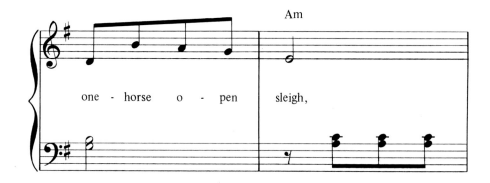

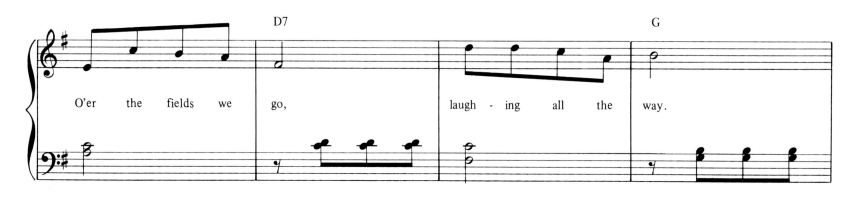

Detail of a color lithograph by Valerie Petter (Austrian, 1881–1963), published by the Wiener Werkstätte, ca. 1908.

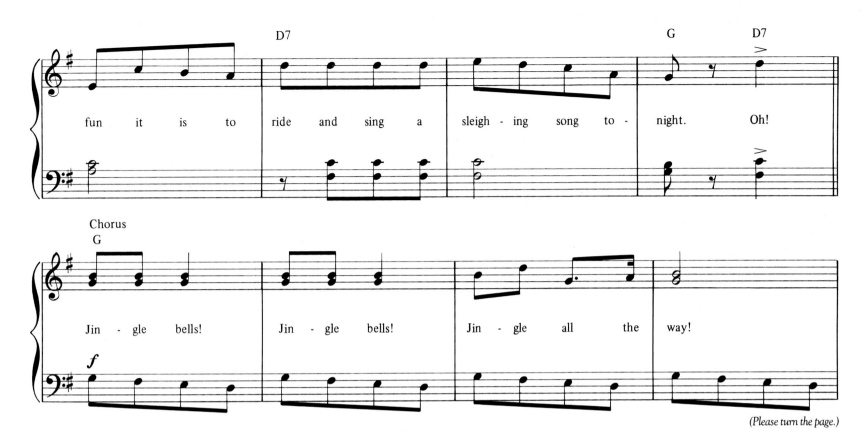

fun it is to ride and sing a sleigh - ing song to - night. Oh!

Chorus

Jin - gle bells! Jin - gle bells! Jin - gle all the way!

(Please turn the page.)

The Sleigh Race. Detail of a hand-colored lithograph published by Currier & Ives, New York, 1859.

Adaptation of drawings in ink and watercolor made for Brewster and Co., New York. American, late 19th century.

SANTA CLAUS IS COMIN' TO TOWN

Words by Haven Gillespie
Music by J. Fred Coots

Moderately

You bet-ter watch out, you better not cry, Bet-ter not pout, I'm tell-ing you why: San-ta Claus is com-in' to town.

He's mak-ing a list and check-ing it twice,

(Please turn the page.)

Santa (detail). Jean Ray, French. Hand-colored illustration from "Conte de Noël," in *La Guirlande: Album d'Art et de Littérature*, published in Paris, 1920.

29

Gon - na find out who's naugh-ty and nice: San - ta Claus is

com - in' to town. He sees you when you're

Woodcut illustrations by Edgard Tijtgat, Belgian, 1879–1957.
From *Le Lendemain de la Saint-Nicolas,*
published by Remy Havermans, Brussels, 1913.

O COME, ALL YE FAITHFUL

Moderately

Words by Frederick Oakeley (English) and John Frances Wade (Latin)
Music by John Reading

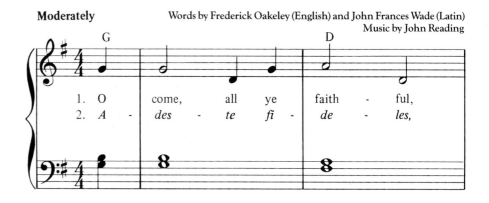

1. O come, all ye faith - ful,
2. A - des - te fi - de - les,

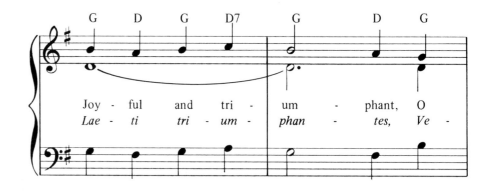

Joy - ful and tri - um - phant, O
Lae - ti tri - um - phan - tes, Ve -

come ye, O come ye, to Beth - le - hem.
ni - te, ve - ni - te in Beth - le - hem.

Come and be - hold Him,
Na - tum vi - de - te,

(Please turn the page.)

Detail of a color lithograph by Josef von Divéky (Austrian, 1887–1951), published by the Wiener Werkstätte, 1908.

Illustration by Jeanne Kerremans (Belgian, active 1930s) from *Le Manteau de Roi et autres Contes de Noël* by Camille Melloy. Published by Desclée, de Brouwer, Brussels, 1939.

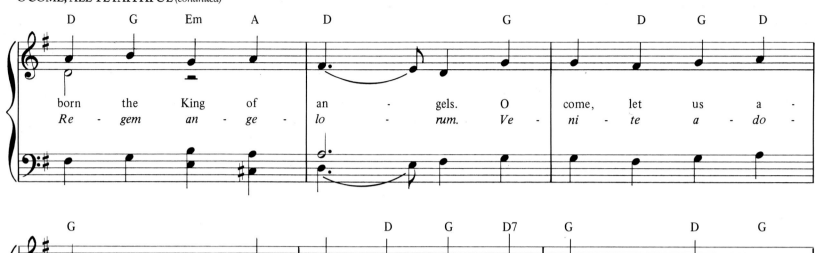

born the King of an - gels. O come, let us a -
Re - gem an - ge - lo - rum. Ve - ni - te a - do -

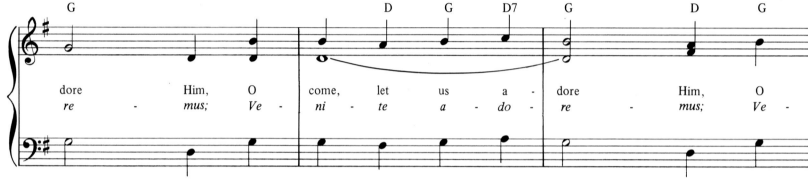

dore Him, O come, let us a - dore Him, O
re - mus; Ve - ni - te a - do - re - mus; Ve -

come, let us a - dore Him, Christ the Lord.
ni - te a - do - re - mus, Do - mi - num.

Additional verses:

3. Sing, choirs of angels,
   Sing in exultation;
   Sing all ye citizens of heav'n above:
   Glory to God in the highest.
   O come, let us adore Him,
   O come, let us adore Him,
   O come, let us adore Him, Christ, the Lord.

4. Yea, Lord, we greet Thee,
   Born this happy morning;
   Jesus, to Thee be glory giv'n;
   Word of the Father, now in flesh appearing.
   O come, let us adore Him,
   O come, let us adore Him,
   O come, let us adore Him, Christ, the Lord.

Detail from a woodcut, *Rest on the Flight into Egypt,* by Lucas Cranach the Elder, German, 1472–1553.

O HOLY NIGHT

Words by John Sullivan Dwight
Music by Adolphe Adam

Slowly, in 2 (♩ = 1 beat)

O ho - ly night,_____ the stars are bright - ly shin - ing; It is the night of the dear Sav - ior's birth._____ Long lay the

(Please turn the page.)

Annunciation to the Shepherds (detail). Henri Rivière, French, 1864–1951. Color lithograph from a broadside for *La Marche à l'Etoile* by Georges Fragerolle.

Nativity with the Annunciation to the Shepherds.
Follower of Jan Joest of
Calcar, Flemish, active by
1505, d. 1519. Oil on wood.

O HOLY NIGHT *(continued)*

(Please turn the page.)

O HOLY NIGHT (*continued*)

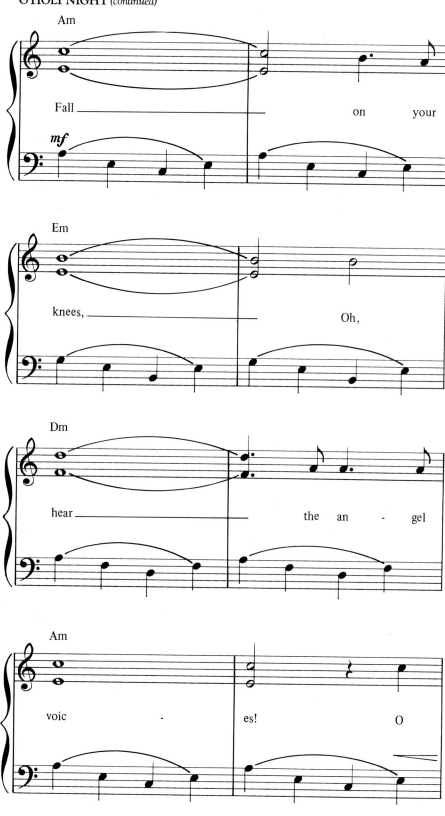

Virgin and Child. Rhenish or Bohemian, first quarter of the 15th century. Wood, polychromed and gilt.

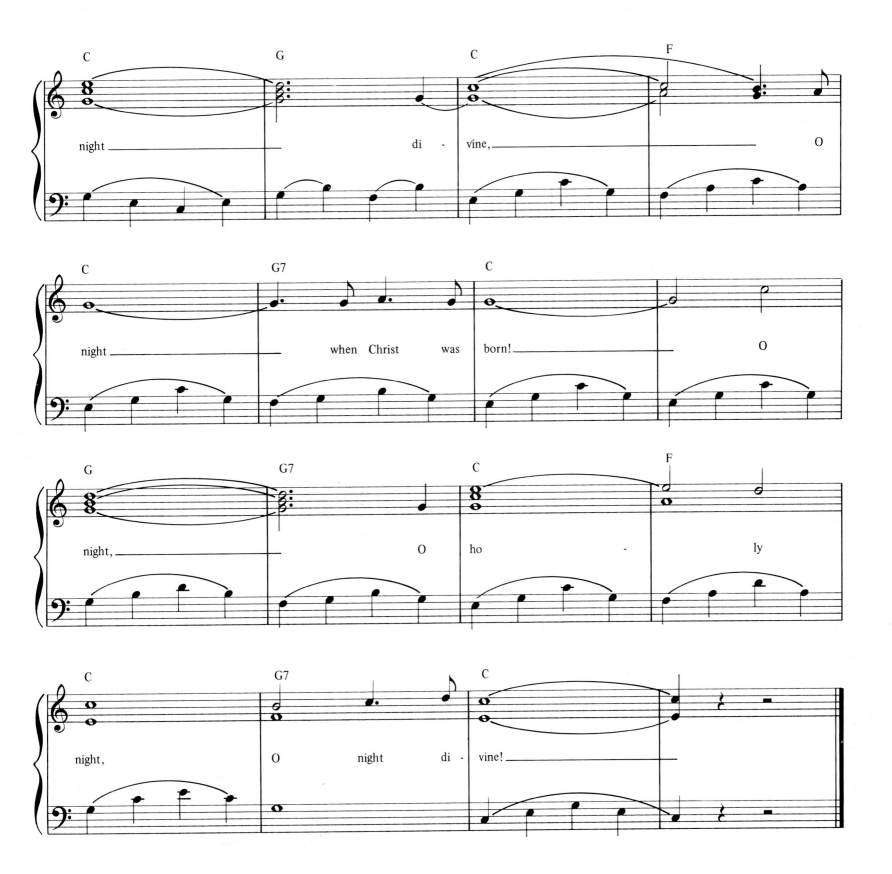

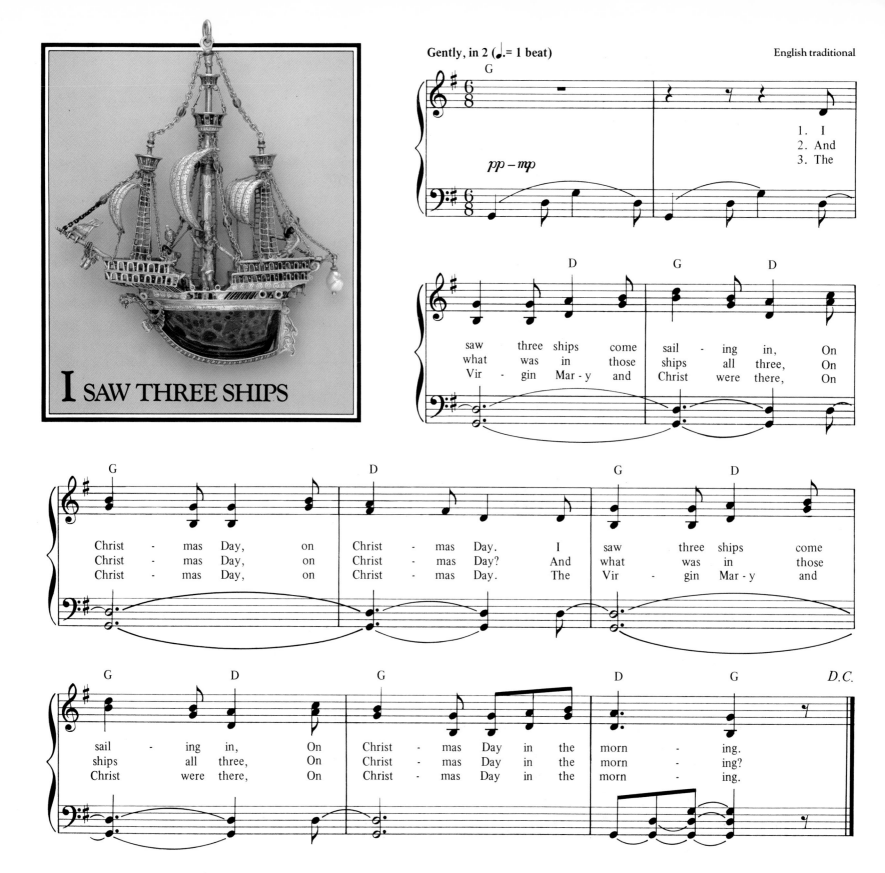

I SAW THREE SHIPS

Gently, in 2 (♩.= 1 beat)   English traditional

1. I
2. And
3. The

saw three ships come sail - ing in, On
what was in those ships all three, On
Vir - gin Mar - y and Christ were there, On

Christ - mas Day, on Christ - mas Day. I
Christ - mas Day, on Christ - mas Day? And
Christ - mas Day, on Christ - mas Day. And

saw three ships come
what was in those
Vir - gin Mar - y and

sail - ing in, On
ships all three, On
Christ were there, On

Christ - mas Day in the morn - ing.
Christ - mas Day in the morn - ing?
Christ - mas Day in the morn - ing.

D.C.

Ship pendant. Probably southern European, second half of the 16th century. Gold, partially enameled, and painted rock crystal, with a pearl.

40

Detail of an illustration by
Francis D. Bedford (British,
1864–1934) for "I Saw Three
Ships," from *A Book of
Nursery Rhymes*, published
by Doubleday & McClure
Co., New York, 1897.

O CHRISTMAS TREE

German traditional

Firmly

1. O Christ-mas tree, O Christ-mas tree, you stand in ver-dant beau-ty. O
2. O Christ-mas tree, O Christ-mas tree, you fill all hearts with gai-ety. O

Christ-mas tree, O Christ-mas tree, you stand in ver-dant beau-ty. Your
Christ-mas tree, O Christ-mas tree, you fill all hearts with gai-ety. On

*Guitar: Capo 3rd fret

(Please turn the page.)

Detail of a color lithograph by Josef von Divéky (Austrian, 1887–1951), published by the Wiener Werkstätte, ca. 1908.

Christmas tree at The Metropolitan Museum of Art. Decorated with dressed figures of polychromed terracotta and wood. Italian (Neapolitan), late 18th–early 19th century.

O CHRISTMAS TREE (continued)

boughs are green in sum-mer's glow, And
Christ-mas Day in you stand so tall, Af-

do not fade in win-ter's snow. O
ford-ing joy to one and all. O

Christ-mas tree, O Christ-mas tree, You
Christ-mas tree, O Christ-mas tree, You

stand in ver-dant beau-ty.
fill all hearts with gai-ety.

Detail of the Christmas tree at The Metropolitan Museum of Art.

WE THREE KINGS OF ORIENT ARE

Words and music by John Henry Hopkins

Moderately flowing

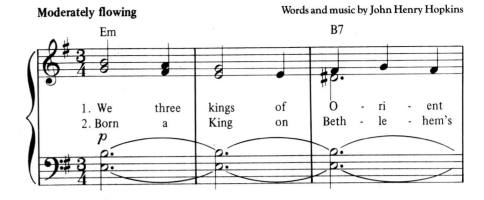

1. We three kings of O - ri - ent
2. Born a King on Beth - le - hem's

are, Bear - ing gifts we
plain, Gold I bring we to

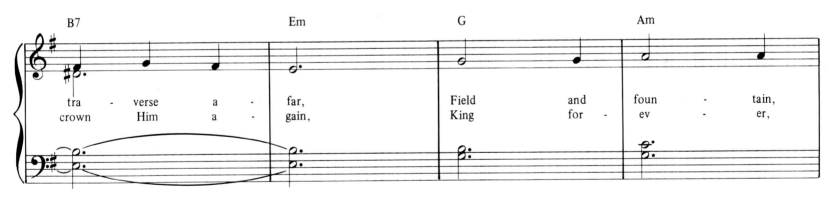

tra - verse a - far, Field and foun - tain,
crown Him a - gain, King for - ev - er,

moor and moun - tain, Fol - low - ing yon - der star.}
ceas - ing nev - er, O - ver us all to reign.}

(Please turn the page.)

The Three Kings. Detail from a tile. Dutch, 18th century. Tin-enameled earthenware.

The Journey of the Magi. Sassetta (Stefano di Giovanni), Italian (Sienese), active by 1423, d. 1450. Tempera and gold on wood.

Additional verses:

3. Frankincense to offer have I,
   Incense owns a Deity nigh.
   Pray'r and praising, all men raising,
   Worship Him, God most high.

   (Chorus)

4. Myrrh is mine, its bitter perfume
   Breathes a life of gathering gloom;
   Sorrowing, sighing, bleeding, dying,
   Sealed in the stone-cold tomb.

   (Chorus)

5. Glorious now behold him arise,
   King and God and sacrifice.
   Alleluia, Alleluia,
   Earth to heav'ns replies.

   (Chorus)

Words by Edmund Hamilton Sears   Music by Richard Storrs Willis

IT CAME UPON THE MIDNIGHT CLEAR

Gently, in 2 (♩.= 1 beat)

1. It came up-on the mid-night clear, that glo-ri-ous song of old, From an - gels bend - ing near the earth to touch their harps of gold. Peace on the earth, good will to men from

2. Still through the clo-ven skies they come, with peace - ful wings un-furl'd; And still their heav'n-ly mu - sic floats o'er all the wea - ry world: A-bove its sad and low - ly plains they

*Guitar: Capo 3rd fret

Dante and Beatrice with the Blessed Souls (detail). Woodcut from *Comedia dell'Inferno, del Purgatorio, e del Paradiso*, by Dante Alighieri. Published by Giovambattista Marchiò Sessa et Fratelli, Venice, 1578.

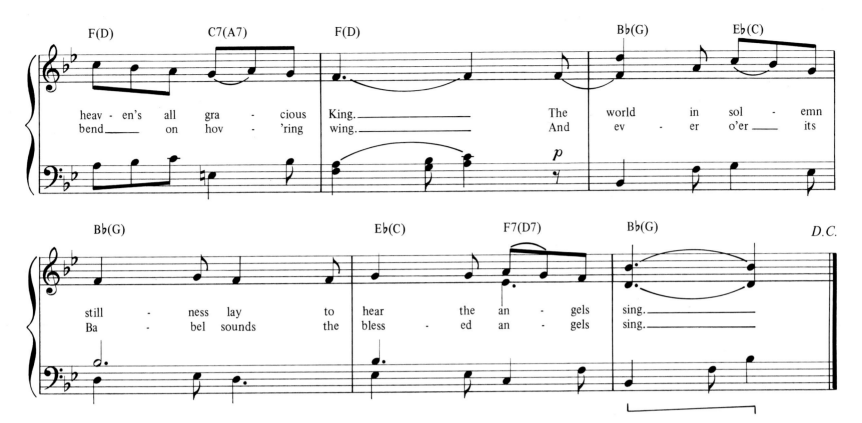

heav - en's all gra - cious King._____ The
bend_____ on hov - 'ring wing._____ And

world in sol - emn
ev - er o'er_____ its

p

still - ness lay to hear the an - gels sing._____
Ba - bel sounds to the bless - ed an - gels sing._____

D.C.

The Way Home (detail). Ludwig Michaelek, Austrian, 1859–1942. Color etching and aquatint, 1901.

WHAT CHILD IS THIS?

Words by William Chatterton Dix
Music traditional ("Greensleeves")

Gently

1. What Child is this, _____ who
2. Why lies He in _____ such
3. So bring Him in - cense,

laid to rest, _____ On
mean es - tate, _____ Where
gold and myrrh; _____ Come,

Mar - y's lap _____ is sleep - ing? Whom
ox and ass _____ are feed - ing? Good
peas - ant king, _____ to own Him. The

an - gels greet _____ with an - thems sweet, _____ While
Chris - tian, fear _____ for sin - ners here, _____ The
King of Kings, _____ sal - va - tion brings; _____ Let

(Please turn the page.)

The Nativity (detail). Woodcut from *Meditations on the Life of Christ.* Italian (Venetian), 1576.

The Adoration of the Magi. Hieronymus Bosch, Flemish, active by 1480, d. 1516. Tempera and oil on wood.

Moderately, rather freely

THE TWELVE DAYS OF CHRISTMAS

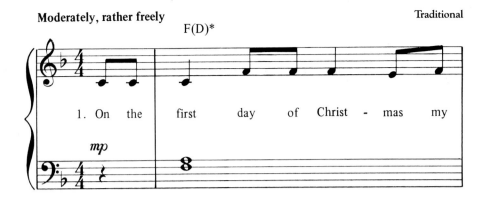

F(D)*

mp

1. On the first day of Christ - mas my

C7(A7)   F(D)

true love sent to me a

B♭(G)   F(D)   C7(A7)   F(D)

par - tridge in a pear tree._____ 2. On the sec - ond day of Christ - mas my

C7(A7)   F(D)   C7(A7)   F(D)   B♭(G)   F(D)   C7(A7)

true love sent to me two tur - tle - doves and a par - tridge in a pear

*Guitar: Capo 3rd fret

(Please turn the page.)

Detail of an illustration from a tournament manuscript. German (Nuremberg), late 16th century. Ink and watercolor with gold.

tree._____ 3. On the third day of Christ - mas my true love sent to me

three French_ hens, two tur - tle - doves, and a par - tridge_ in a pear

tree._____ 4. On the fourth day of Christ - mas my true love sent to me

four call - ing birds, three French_ hens, two tur - tle - doves, and a

(*Please turn the page.*)

Embroidered textile. English, first half of the 17th century. Silk on canvas.

par - tridge— in a pear tree._____ 5. On the fifth day of Christ - mas my

Broadly

true love sent to me five gold - en rings,

Briskly, as before

four— call - ing birds,

three French hens, two— tur-tle - doves, and a par - tridge— in a pear tree._____ 6. On the

Adaptation of a color lithograph by Rudolf Kalvack (Austrian, 1883–1932), published by the Wiener Werkstätte, ca. 1908.

THE FIRST NOEL

Moderately

English traditional

mf

1. The first No - el the an - gel did say, Was to certain poor shep - herds in fields as they lay; In
2. They look - ed up and saw a star shin - ing in the east be - yond them far; And
3. And by the light of that same star Three wise men came from coun - try far; To

fields where they lay keep - ing their sheep On a
to the earth it gave great light tent, And
seek for a king was their in - And to

(Please turn the page.)

Detail of a color lithograph by Oscar Kokoschka (Austrian, 1886–1980), published by the Wiener Werkstätte, 1906–08.

Annunciation to the Shepherds. Detail from a wool tapestry. German (Upper Rhine), late 15th century.

Chorus

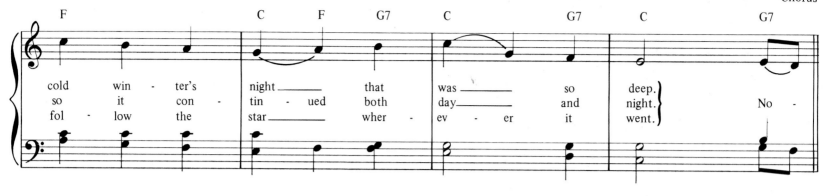

cold   win - ter's   night_____ that   was_____ so   deep. }
so   it   con - tin - ued   that   both   day_____ and   night. }   No -
fol - low   the   star_____ wher - ev - er   it   went. }

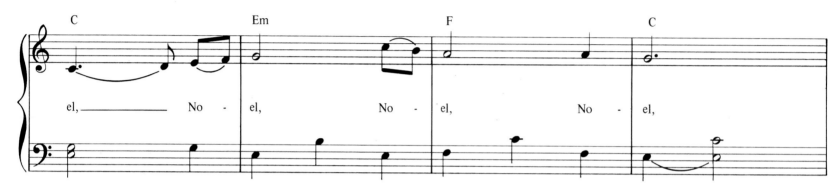

el,_____ No - el,   No - el,   No - el,

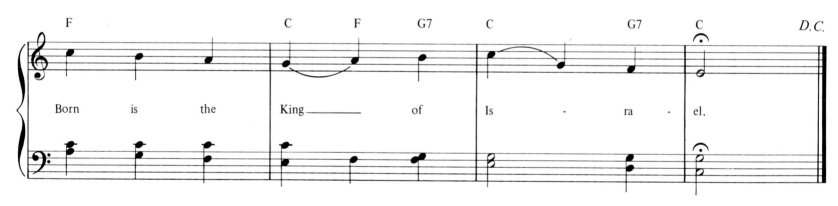

Born   is   the   King_____ of   Is - ra - el.

D.C.

Two angels. Detail from an undyed linen and wool tapestry curtain. Egyptian (Coptic), 6th century.

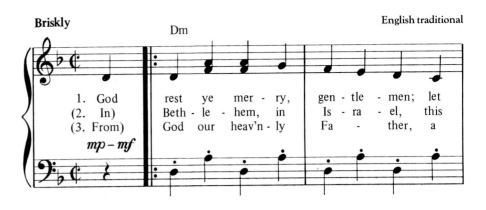

Briskly

Dm

English traditional

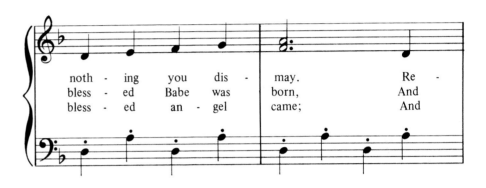

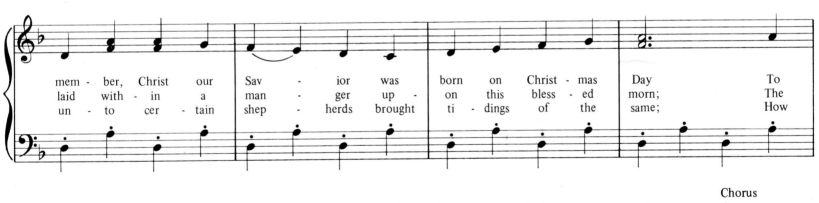

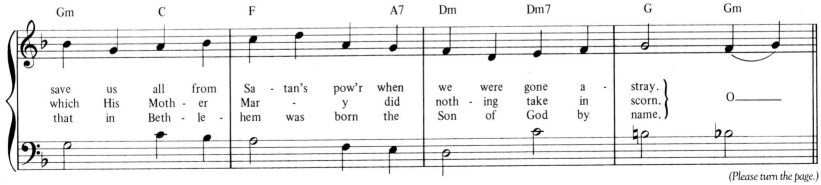

(Please turn the page.)

Woodcut by Allen Lewis, American, 1873–1957.

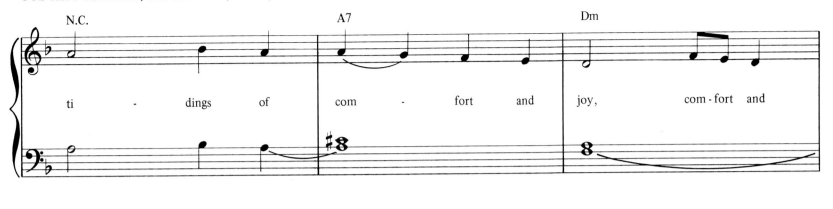

ti - dings of com - fort and joy, com - fort and

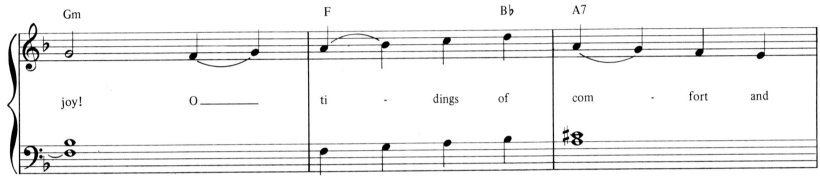

joy! O _____ ti - dings of com - fort and

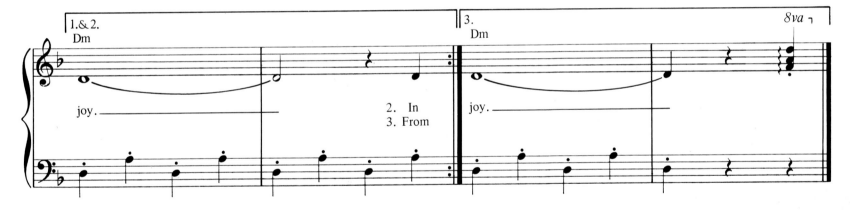

joy. _____ 2. In 3. From joy. _____

The Nativity. Center panel from a triptych by Gerard David, Flemish, active by 1484, d. 1523. Tempera and oil on canvas, transferred from wood.

Detail of an illuminated manuscript page from the *Belles Heures* of Jean, Duke of Berry. Jean, Pol, and Herman de Limbourg, French (Paris), active ca. 1400–1416. Tempera and gold on vellum.

Good
KING WENCESLAS

Words by John Mason Neale
Music traditional

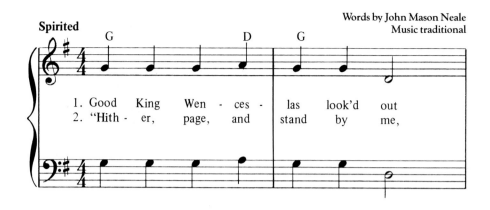

Spirited

G   D   G

1. Good   King   Wen - ces - las   look'd   out
2. "Hith - er,   page, and   stand   by   me,

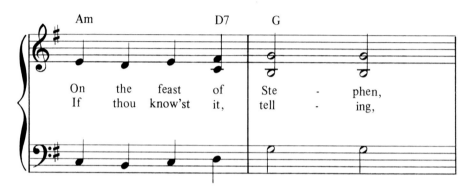

Am   D7   G

On   the   feast   of   Ste - phen,
If   thou know'st it,   tell - ing,

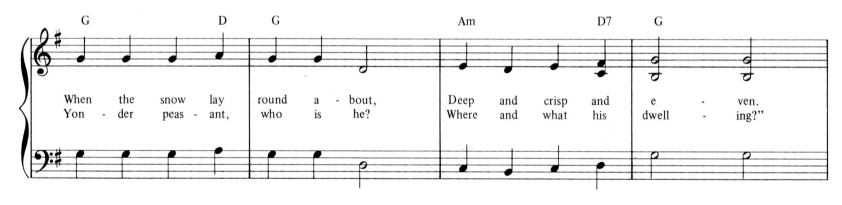

G   D   G   Am   D7   G

When   the   snow   lay   round a - bout,   Deep   and   crisp   and   e - ven.
Yon - der   peas - ant,   who   is   he?   Where   and   what   his   dwell - ing?"

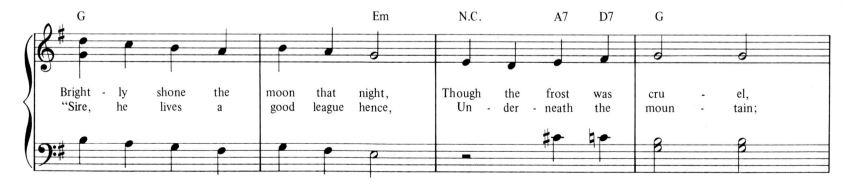

G   Em   N.C.   A7   D7   G

Bright - ly   shone   the   moon   that   night,   Though   the   frost   was   cru - el,
"Sire,   he   lives   a   good   league   hence,   Un - der - neath   the   moun - tain;

Details of two color lithographs by Carl Krenek (Austrian, 1880–1948), published by the Wiener Werkstätte, ca. 1912.

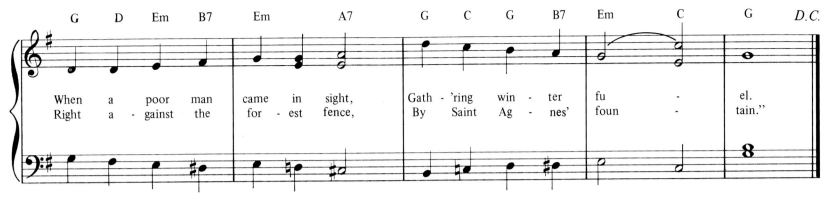

When a poor man came in sight, Gath-'ring winter fu - el.
Right a - gainst the for - est fence, By Saint Ag - nes' foun - tain."

Additional verses:

3. "Bring me flesh and bring me wine,
   Bring me pine logs hither.
   Thou and I will see him dine,
   When we bear him thither."
   Page and monarch forth they went,
   Forth they went together,
   Through the rude wind's wild lament,
   And the bitter weather.

4. "Sire, the night is darker now,
   And the wind blows stronger.
   Fails my heart, I know not how,
   I can go no longer."
   "Mark my footsteps, my good page,
   Tread thou in them boldly.
   Thou shalt find the winter's rage
   Freeze thy blood less coldly."

5. In his master's steps he trod,
   When the snow lay dinted.
   Heat was in the very sod
   Which the Saint had printed.
   Therefore, Christian men, be sure,
   Wealth or rank possessing,
   Ye who now will bless the poor,
   Shall yourselves find blessing.

ANGELS WE HAVE HEARD ON HIGH

French traditional

Joyously

1. An - gels we have heard on high, Sweet - ly sing - ing
2. Shep - herds, why this ju - bi - lee? Why your joy - ous
3. Come to Beth - le - hem and see Him whose birth the

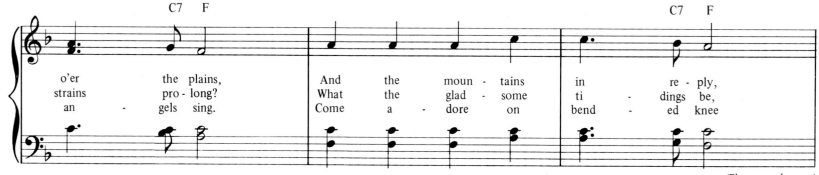

o'er the plains, And the moun - tains in re - ply,
strains pro - long? What the glad - some ti - dings be,
an - gels sing. Come a - dore on bend - ed knee

(Please turn the page.)

Detail of a color lithograph by Franz Karl Delavilla
(Austrian, 1884–1967), published by the Wiener Werkstätte, 1908.

Annunciation to the Shepherds. Illuminated manuscript page from the *Belles Heures* of Jean, Duke of Berry.
Jean, Pol, and Herman de Limbourg, French (Paris), active ca. 1400–1416. Tempera and gold on vellum.

eus in ad
iutorium
meum in
tende.

Domine ad adiu
uandum me festina.
Gloria patri et filio
et spiritu sancto.

ANGELS WE HAVE HEARD ON HIGH *(continued)*

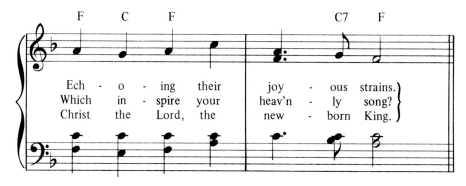

Ech - o - ing their joy - ous strains.}
Which in - spire your heav'n - ly song?}
Christ the Lord, the new - born King.}

Chorus

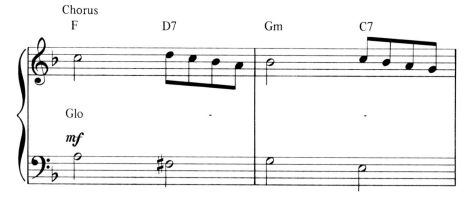

Glo - -

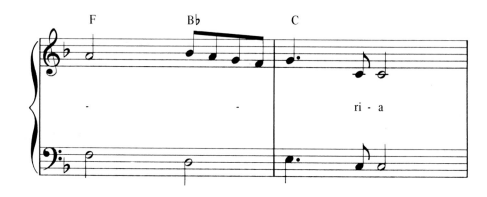

- - ri - a

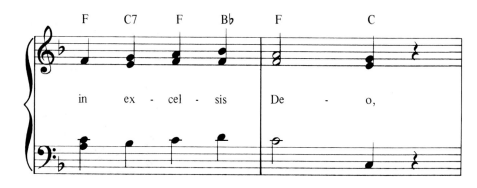

in ex - cel - sis De - o,

Glo - -

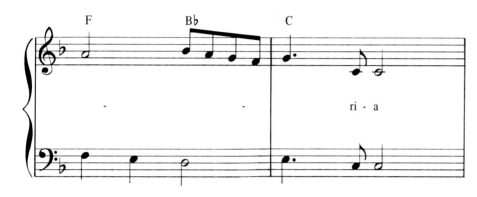

- - ri - a

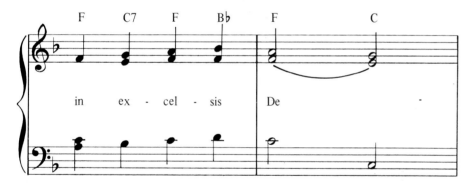

in ex - cel - sis De -

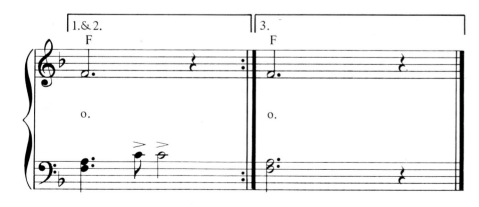

1.& 2.

3.

o.

o.

Detail of a border design by Aubrey Beardsley (British, 1872–1898)
for *Le Morte d'Arthur* by Sir Thomas Malory, 1893–94. Drawing in ink on paper.

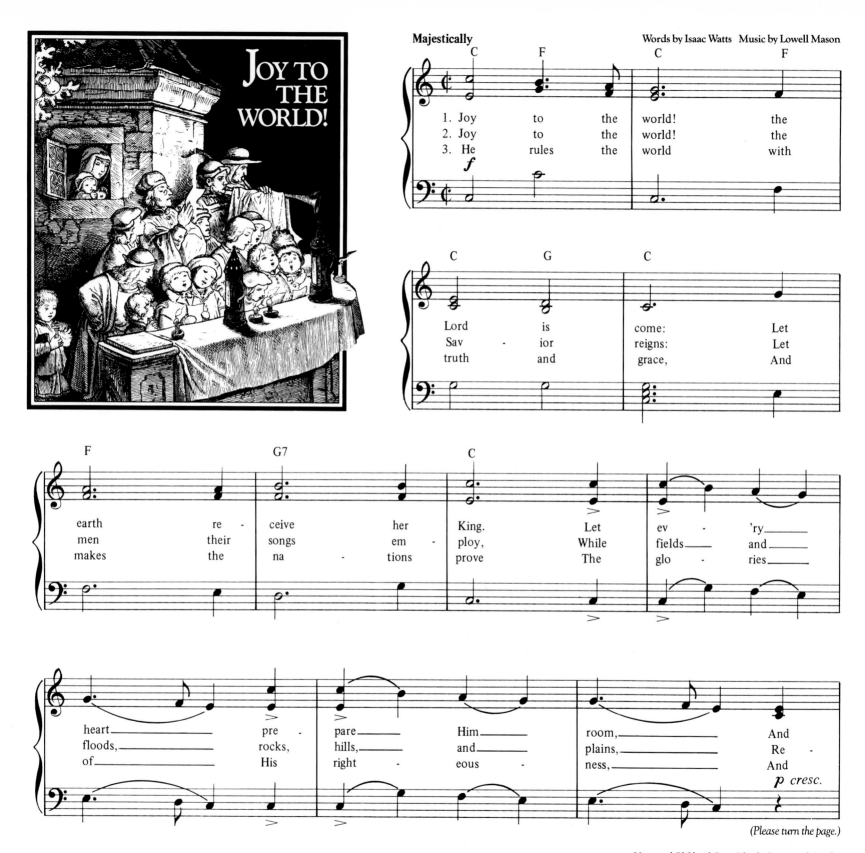

Majestically

Words by Isaac Watts   Music by Lowell Mason

| C | F | C | F |

f

1. Joy to the world! the
2. Joy to the world! the
3. He rules the world with

| C | G | C |

Lord is come: Let
Sav - ior reigns: Let
truth and grace, And

| F | G7 | C |

earth re ceive her King. Let ev - - 'ry
men their songs em - ploy, While The fields and
makes the na - tions prove glo - ries

heart pre pare Him room, And
floods, rocks, hills, and plains, Re -
of His right - eous - ness, And

p cresc.

(Please turn the page.)

Christmas Carolers (detail). Ludwig Richter, German, 1803–1884. Wood engraving.

Virgin and Child with Saint John the Baptist and Angels.
François Boucher, French, 1703–1770. Oil on canvas, 1765.

Detail from a woodcut, *Rest on the Flight into Egypt,* by Lucas Cranach the Elder, German, 1472–1553.

WE WISH YOU A MERRY CHRISTMAS

English traditional

Joyfully

1. We wish you a Mer - ry Christ - mas, We
2. Oh, bring us a fig - gy pud - ding, Oh,
3. We won't go un - til we've got some, We

wish you a Mer - ry Christ - mas, We
bring us a fig - gy pud - ding, Oh,
won't go un - til we've got some, We

wish you a Mer - ry Christ - mas and a Hap - py New Year. Good
bring us a fig - gy pud - ding and a cup of good cheer.
won't go un - til we've got some so____ bring some good out here.

Chorus

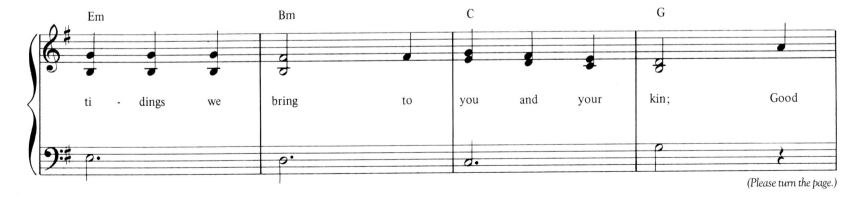

ti - dings we bring to you and your kin; Good

(*Please turn the page.*)

Christmas-Time (The Blodgett Family). Eastman Johnson, American, 1824–1906. Oil on canvas, 1864.

Illustrations by Arthur Rackham (British, 1867–1939) for *Cinderella*, retold by C. S. Evans. Published by William Heinemann, London, and J. B. Lippincott Co., Philadelphia, 1919.

AULD LANG SYNE

Moderately

Words by Robert Burns
Music traditional

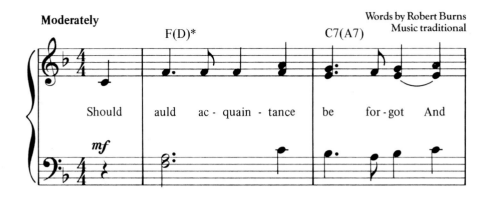

Should auld ac - quain - tance be for - got And

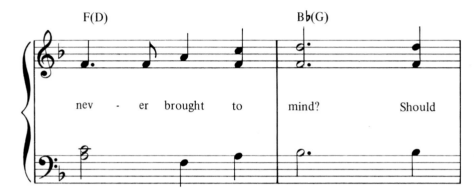

nev - er brought to mind? Should

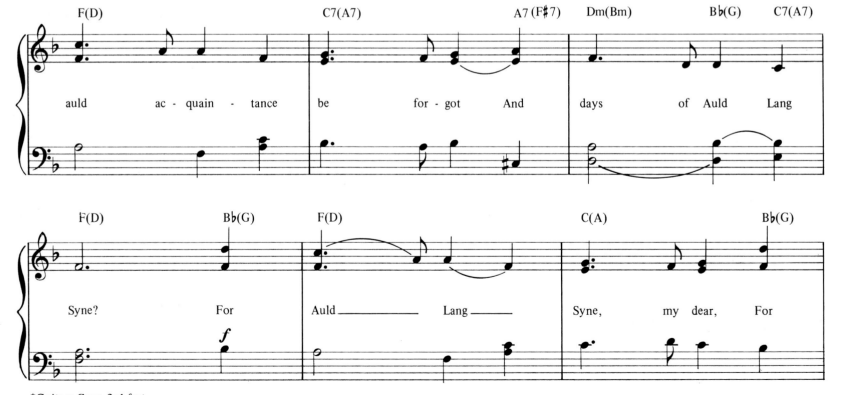

auld ac - quain - tance be for - got And days of Auld Lang

Syne? For Auld _____ Lang _____ Syne, my dear, For

*Guitar: Capo 3rd fret

Detail of a color lithograph published by the Wiener Werkstätte, ca. 1914.

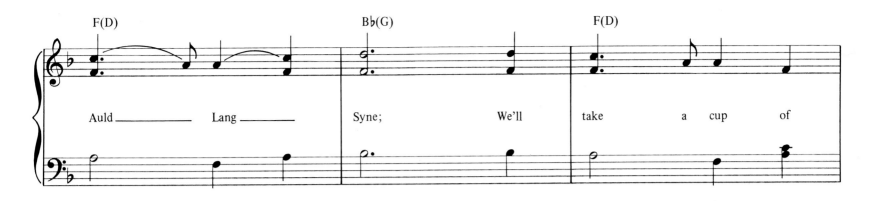

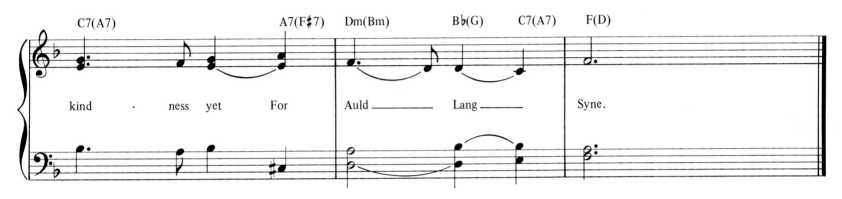

Adaptation from *The Marriage Feast at Cana*. Anders Pålsson, Swedish, 1781–1849. Painted linen wall hanging, 1818.

CREDITS

Front cover:
Arents Collections, The New York Public Library

Back cover:
Thomas J. Watson Library, Rogers Fund, 1922

Title page and endpapers:
Gift of David W. Cugell, M.D., 1985   1985.1148.7

Page 3:
Gift of David W. Cugell, M.D., 1985   1985.1148.8

Page 4:
Private collection

Page 6:
The Cloisters Collection, 1937   37.52.6

Page 7:
Francis L. Leland Fund, 1913   13.64.4

Page 8:
Harris Brisbane Dick Fund, 1931   31.65

Page 9:
The Jack and Belle Linsky Collection, 1982   1982.60.47

Page 10:
Harris Brisbane Dick Fund, by exchange, 1942   42.26.1

Page 11:
Gift of J. Pierpont Morgan, 1917   17.190.3

Page 12:
Gift of May Dougherty King, 1983   1983.490

Page 13:
The Cloisters Collection, 1958   58.71b

Page 14:
The Cloisters Collection, 1958   58.71a

Page 15:
Harris Brisbane Dick Fund, 1938   38.38.7

Page 16:
Museum Accession, 1943

Page 17:
Gift of Bessie Potter Vonnoh, 1941   41.12.84

Page 18:
The New York Public Library

Page 19:
Gift of Mrs. John S. Lamont, 1974   1974.669

Page 20:
Museum Accession, 1943

Pages 21 and 22:
Rogers Fund, 1970   1970.544.1

Page 24:
The Friedsam Collection, Bequest of Michael Friedsam,
1931   32.100.343

Page 25:
Rogers Fund, 1906   06.1214

Page 26:
Museum Accession, 1943

Page 27:
Bequest of Adele S. Colgate, 1962   63.550.254

Page 28:
Gift of William Brewster, 1923
23.112.1221, 1231, 1254, 1457

Page 29:
Thomas J. Watson Library, Rogers Fund, 1922

Page 30:
Harris Brisbane Dick Fund, 1930   30.96.8

Page 32:
Museum Accession, 1943

Page 33:
Gift of C. Whitney Dall, Jr., in Memory of Emily M. Dall,
1976   1976.625.3

Page 34:
Gift of Felix Warburg and his family, 1941   41.1.159

Page 35:
The Elisha Whittelsey Collection, The Elisha Whittelsey Fund,
1966   66.559.65

Page 36:
The Jack and Belle Linsky Collection, 1982   1982.60.22

Page 38:
Anonymous Loan

Page 40:
The Friedsam Collection, Bequest of Michael Friedsam,
1931   32.100.312

Page 41:
The Elisha Whittelsey Collection, The Elisha Whittelsey Fund,
1966   66.540.2

Page 42:
Museum Accession, 1943

Pages 43 and 44:
Gift of Loretta Hines Howard, 1964   64.164.1–167

Page 45:
Museum Accession, X.158

Page 47:
Maitland F. Griggs Collection, Bequest of Maitland F. Griggs,
1943   43.98.1

Page 48:
Gift of Francis Leonard Cater, 1958   58.584

Page 49:
Rogers Fund, 1923   23.52.12 (4)

Page 50:
Rogers Fund, 1922   22.73.3–176 (9)

Page 51:
John Stewart Kennedy Fund, 1912   13.26

Page 53:
Rogers Fund, 1922   959.4 T64

Page 55:
Gift of Irwin Untermyer, 1964   64.101.1305

Pages 56 and 58:
Museum Accessions, 1943

Page 59:
Gift of Charles F. Iklé, 1957   57.126

Page 60:
Rogers Fund, 1912   12.182.45

Page 61:
Gift of Estate of John Taylor Arms, 1955   55.621.157

Page 62:
The Jules Bache Collection, 1949   49.7.20b

Page 63:
The Cloisters Collection, 1954   54.1.1

Pages 64, 65, and 66:
Museum Accessions, 1943

Page 67:
The Cloisters Collection, 1954   54.1.1

Pages 68 and 69:
Rogers Fund, 1923   23.90

Page 70:
Rogers Fund, 1921   21.89

Page 71:
Gift of Adelaide Milton de Groot, in memory of the de Groot
and Hawley families, 1966   66.167

Page 72:
Gift of Felix Warburg and his family, 1941   41.1.159

Page 73:
Gift of Juliet W. Robinson, 1918   18.77

Page 74:
Gift of Mr. and Mrs. Stephen Whitney Blodgett,
1983   1983.486

Page 75:
Bequest of Glenn Tilley Morse, 1950   50.602.1448

Page 76:
Museum Accession, 1943

Page 77:
Gift of Mr. and Mrs. William Maxwell Evarts, 1953   53.98

Page 79:
Museum Accession, 1943

Page 80:
Purchase, Rogers Fund and Funds from Various Donors, 1976
1976.177

INDEX OF FIRST LINES

GUITAR CHORD DIAGRAMS

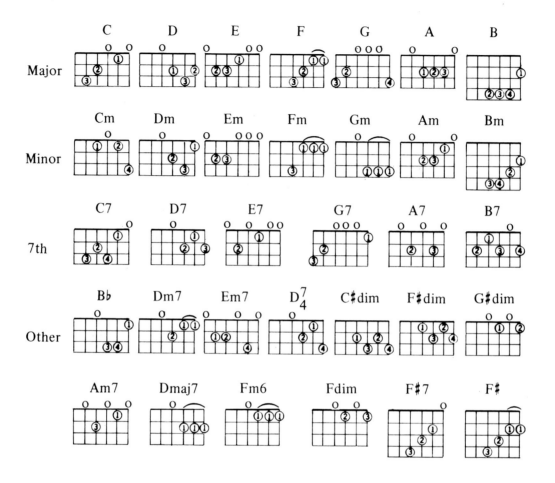